A STAR IS REBORN

ATHARVA HANMALWAR

Contents

Contents

Contents

Preface

The book " A star is reborn" is series of emotions that catalises a shades of life. As the seasons change we adapt diffeerently. Similarly different poems of soldiers, love ,death and so on....it consists.
It draws the cosmos, and the universe in poem and being happy.

All that is that you feel what you are and more,
All that you see is What this world is and more;
That's when you know who you are,
When everything is dark around you be the bright light of your own darkness,

When you will find you will break or fall apart.
Hold yourself strong, motivate yourself to move ahead,
You will know that you are at the best version of your life .

ONE

OCEAN

As i look from the edge of ocean,
A glimmering and resonating golden rays,
Of sun appeared as dawn;
So many waves coming towards me,
So many creatures with hills and fins,
The waves, were splashing closer,
As i realise the world as bigger,
The waves , whispers to the soft sand,
The water sweeps over my feet surrounds where I stand;
It smell the salty air around me as you see you will love it more than others too;
When the waves heats the rocks and again return back to the floor;
You will find your peace, right there;

TWO

THE NAME OF BIRD

You will find a downy woodpecker in the snow,
I was in the frosty house, where the wooden flank, was out;
There was a deer approach house near the strip yew leaves;
Inthe corridor at the entrance;
There was a woody tree near to house,
It was dark, and gloom bunch of leaves,
Cherries oak and berry was too there?
Deer grinned at woodpecker with jade disk of slate;
I called pecker,but the name doesn't listen by pecker;
There was dark every where and the snowfall starts;
The bird moved out to woody tree and sal,
At night I googled the word "woodpecker"
The result shown many species
With different names;

THREE

LINES WRITTEN ON ARAVALLI

O Aravalli you are the sister of vindhya and western ghats
of Sahayadri,
The pave mates at the foothills created by the soil,
Your enigmatic beauty has robbed my heart,
O great Himalayas, the father of all you are so tall;
Your footprints of son and daughter all over the world,
Your daughter's has oracles of thousands of one,
Which was a lofted with aroma of essence,
A magenta of leaves with beautiful flowers and trees,
The kingdom of species and young animals services with
you;

FOUR

THE TREE

I have spend my time creating stories and evolving in the
beauty of nature,
Where there was branches, valley and rivers and forests by
my side;
A reindeer coming by my side,
I was a lofted with dreams of nature,
The deer came and stopped looking with mystery eye;
As the winter, came asking for deer sigh,
He ran in the wild, with muse sound and stopped as the
hunter stops fire,

I sat near my favourite tree, where there was peace,
The tree was so big, i have never passed through the branch
of leaf,
It was too high,
Though I have seen the trunk it was so big and giant,
The tree was near the waterfall were, there was divine peace
and freshness in air,
The air soothing my soul, as i have spent time creating,
Stories of Angels dawn on earth

FIVE

MIRRORS

I like mirrors not for what they show,
But for what they hide;
They don't show the vast hollow void in you,
They hide from your own abyss,
they conceal the infinite depths, like the good poetries do;
They hide a lot , but until you look deep into the eyes that
are watching you,
Only until you un look the door by keys,
that you didn't know existed to you;
Then you find yourself looking straight into what dwells in
your void,
It is not light,not darkness;
It is nothing,or just wisdoms of words,
Or nothing from universe appeared;
Or a silent river can see the waves are fluctuating,
Creating something,not to be silent, but creative;

SIX

LIGHT YEARS

We float across space and time,
With freedom of sky and uncountable space,
We float across the cosmos that seeks the home in galaxies,

We keep on moving from constellations to bursting stars,
And meet at the space & time,
We crash in our dreams,
We do not orbit across the rings,
Refusing any planet to be our master,
We wander without strings pulling us back,
Bolting to those universe which are beyond our destiny;
Blinking the darkness while we see each other a millions
light years away;

Where constellations are counting protons,
We are in the planets, were darkness and brightness can be
seen;

We are always close to each other,
Still we are tied with knot of universe,
Till the universe will not destroyed,

We are there together, forever;

SEVEN
WAR

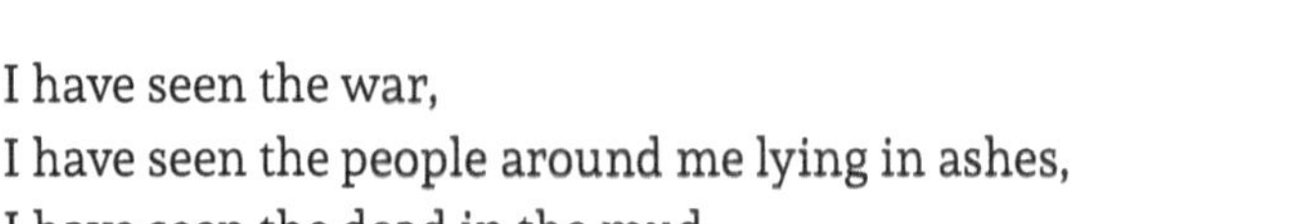

I have seen the war,
I have seen the people around me lying in ashes,
I have seen the dead in the mud,
With people's running out blood and some gotta wounded;

I have seen the cities been destroyed,
Have seen children crying for there father,

When they will come?

I have seen the women's and wives are waiting for their husbands,

When they will come??
The flowers fell on dead bodies with sadness of Rip,
I have seen some lost there hand, some lost there home,
We were in spiti valleys of mountains,
Were there was dark around,
With silence and thunderstrikes,

Granites were blasted and bullets were wasted,

I have seen the dead night,
Were so many died,
Some lost there control, some lost due to dilemma,

Anxiety was seen in the mob,
Dead bodies were lying in the floors,
There was terror and threat around us for all,
There was undulated faces of youngster,
I have seen some people writes the pages with blood;

EIGHT
THE GANGES

A mystical flow from Himalayas,
Waves as deep, leap out to reach,

A luminous haze our water,
And snow covered mountain top in heaven,
Some secret river lies,
Stirring not earthward this river of the gods,
It flows quiet and slow laps Varanasi shores,
Holy songs reverberate emanating from floating boats,
The sacred river continues to flow,
Gangacs pace is calm & slow,

Floating lamps set water a glows
burning camphor's hazy smoke;
Evening prayers deluge of faith
A millions heads a millions breaths,

Soggy flower ,offerings washed ashore,
Ganga flow calm and slow,
Priests chants a lonch shells
Murmur a prayer take a dip atone for their worldly sins and

then return to commit some more Ganga flow gentle and snow;

NINE
THE AUTUMN SEASON

As imperceptibly of lushy green grass,
Lapsed by Autumn leaf falls to see like perfidy,

Noathed like pigment grass associated with coconuts;
Green herbs hides the flower in it's beds,
The nature soothes every drop as cluster of evergreen tree,
Pinned the view, of cuckoo bird;
Toad turns to frog and monkey whistles the rain,
As we wish the nature bless,
As you gathered the vowels of paths,
Sunshines reflects the flower as moath,

The leafy leaves sails to the lake,
And white Husky, comes to the garland,
The blue river changes it to green,
The oak turns to pine & pine turns to oaks,
The butterfly welcomes the season,
As sun shines as bright,
As heavenly light to all,

TEN
PAPER BOATS

At rainy days, i float my paperboats one by one down in the
running stream;
In big letters i write my name on them and the address of
my house,

I hope that someone in some strange land will find them
and know who I am;

During rainy season, I launch my paperboats and look up
into the sky and see the little clouds settling their white
bulging sail"

I race my paperboats with my friends,
We use to play, and paper boat goes from stream to river
then it get invisible;

I dream at night, it was reached on land,
Where there is great person on land,
Who teaches the meaning of life,
Who will asks the life of people is happiness, love and
affection;

ELEVEN
O HIMALAYAS

O Himalayas, o Rampart;
You are the realm of land,
Bowing down my head before you,
The sky kisses your forehead,
The clouds honour you as proud,
Your valleys became abode of Man's Ancestors;
Your signs, your edges doesn't show old ages,
You are young as midst of day& night alteration;
Your peaks are matching with the pleiades in elegance,
Though you are standing on earth,
Your abode is sky's expanse;
Every flowering bud is swinging,
With intoxication of existence,

The brook is melodious descending from highland,
Were bird waving in air,
The sky goes pink, as it blushes in winter
The sun goes pink,as it blushes in winter,
The sun goes red as tomato to see the mountain,
O Himalayas, you are great,
The stories are less to entitle you,

You are the forehead of our land,
You are the victorious cliff of northern land,

TWELVE
THE NIGHT UNDER OAK TREE

The leaves and tassels of the oak,
Were golden green with may,
Pavilion forever broke as round delay,
A Carol like a glory came ,
From topmost twig astir,
Tree was glad as paradise,
As I reach to topmost notch;

The entire star's we see,
We see a wildhthroat oriole,
As a hymn of lily grace,

Plumes get ready with flags,
As white to green,
We continues the fest, with bonafire
Under the tree,

The trees blushes by falling leaves in ground,
The night is cool & calm,

The forest whispers poems& stories of love and kind

THIRTEEN
QUOTE

Love is nothing but an essence of emotions, feelings to express someone

I will make you my Heartbeat
I will make you my heartbeat,
Where the love is preserved Underground,
Where you are with me forever & ever,
As the strings gotta attached to the clothes,
We bind with the thread of hopes,
Which is strong by both sides,
My love is pure for you as white flower glows,
My heart pumps up as you get closer,to me;

My heart strucks as you near by me as numb,
A soft nature of your's always glad my thoughts,
To tell the function of my heart,
It connects like a sparkled wire,
There is the graces, there is the letters,
Which I have been written,

The poems asks me when you will say that you are in love,

You will tell to her,
You are not just friend but a heartbeat of mine

FOURTEEN
IN COLD BLOOD

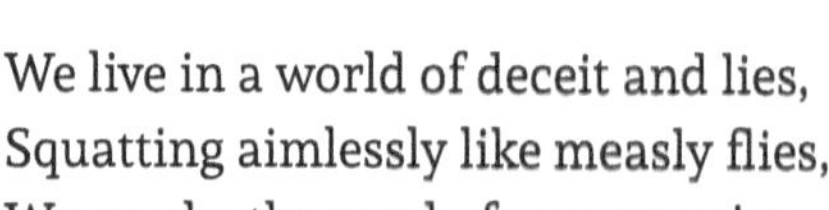

We live in a world of deceit and lies,
Squatting aimlessly like measly flies,
We smoke the need of compromise,
We abuse the ages of the wise,

We spew the venom of hate and greed,
To the winds of change, we pay no need,
The Monster of our invade our souls,
In our sphere of solace, they prickle a hole,

We massage our ego & attitude we fall endlessly from our summit of solitude,
Truth and sincerity burn into heaps of Ashes ,
As Humanity is whipped with millions of lashes,
Loves lies at the crossroads of our wars of hate,
Silently enduring it's misserable fate,
The ghosts of our past lie in wait,
To trap us in cage of cynicism like fish in a boat,
In cold blood we have murdered our sensibilities and goodness,
For we are the accused , the victim and the witness,

The court of eternal justice with God ,
If we are ready to wash the stains of our crime,
And feel the essence our purpose like a musical chime,
In the assume of a assemblage with renaissance of a sage;

FIFTEEN
EQUATIONS

The moon isn't looking for solutions,
The path is accustomed with treachery and lies,
Still we balance our life,
Some solutions isn't enough for us,
It creates hate and anger,
We review our thoughts and got lost in the past stories,
Which weakens us, from inside the soul,
For all these relations, there is one equation,
Which soothes and make happy about life,
Were the bones recreate the enigma of Assurances,
Our heart calms to the Nirvana,
And the street lights spread light around darkness ,
As our mind, freshness our soul;

SIXTEEN

LOST IN SPACE

I was in the search of moon& finally I reached at the natural satelite it was moon. At reaching on moon I was safely landed on the craters of moon. There were two friends one was Astronaut Arthur and other was Astronaut stecy.

We three have landed softly. There was frozen ice which was covered with sand.
We moved some miles away to see things but there was nothing too see only cleft mountains and frozen appearance.

There was earth far miles away. We have seen the sun but we were at the North pole. Were no light comes at the land.

We took the sample of sand by reducing the sand and putted on rover. The rover detected the soil and given result that their is presence of living creatures in a tiny form by the supervision lens.

In the search of life,or any other substances we will get we moved to the top of the hill to see any creatures are present in these ice or not.

We reached at the point where there were several routes but no any sign to get out from these mountain.
We moved from several routes but nothing we get to move out from these icy crystal mountains.

After 30minutes later of struggle our navigation got defected and our oxygen was going to deplete.
We were alone at the mountains. Unfortunately, the rover was unable to come at a peak.

We were lost at space were no one was present.
We signaled the position of us to the headquarters at L.A..
But there was no chances to come out.
We tried every tricks and tips but noone of it work. Stacy was trying to get out of ice so we go to a narrow path and moved slowly under the ice but the time was against us. It closed the door of returning and unfortunately we got stuck and we got lost in space .
Coz all locations got stopped, AI got stopped. Hence we came to the last hour of life were life was struggling and juggling in the space .

SEVENTEEN
LOOKING AT THE HORIZONS

I step in, I step into the world outside,
A linear path, leading to the other,
All homes to their twist, turns and edges,
They ask me what I bring along
My aims, my stains or just me,

So I look around in my attempt to see that surrounds,
I see no chirp, no birds
I splash on the sands, for I see no water
I talk to myself, for i see no people

Yet I hear no sound to the ear and fondless with hair that
tickles,
And it's familiar
It's familiar, coz it's home,
A home just desperate to explore

So I step out again,
I look at the vast horizons

Not because I can
But it make me to explore,

Were sands are smooth with astonishing red,

EIGHTEEN
THE LAST LETTER

I was wandering in lofty Himalayas,
At the trek I found a page was hidden under the stone,
I left out the stone, aside and seen the letter was written,

It was old dusted with brown pages,
As treasury map,
But it was letter of an soldier,
O sweetheart, o dear I am in the rough terrains,
Were life is impossible to leave,
The limbsay not work, the eyes may flatter,
The blood may gotta cold, there is noone to tell the truth,

That we are only five, who resists in fight,
And 20 men's have already dead,

But how long, we will leave i don't know,
But don't tell my mother his son got died,
Don't tell my sister his brother got died,
Don't tell my younger brother that his brother is not alive,

They can't bare the pain, if you know,

If you know I am dead , just don't cry for my sake,
Coz, a man born to die,

It will be tough times for you and everyone,
But you are so strong, that you an hold our family strong,

Don't be panic, or nervous coz, you are the lioness of our house,

NINETEEN
SPARROW SONG IN A CHORUS

Come on, sing a song in a chorus,
We shall pray to bless for all of us,
We are one and unite the kingdom,
You can join us to be our member,

Birds echoes with vowels,
Animals dances with beats,
Ties the beauty of our land,
Peacock pick the feather with twisting hand,

Flute speaks, the rythmn of sound,
Wind want to shoutout a loud,
Berry tree, lavishes with wooden tree,
With tranquish amber as flowers three,

Melodies out, greenery sprouts
Touches the carpet of our mother earth,
The birds chirps and owl hoots,
We come to sing a song in a chorus,

TWENTY
DAY AND NIGHT

Day and night come
Hand in hand like boy and girl,
Passing, chasing, running,
Walking the journeys of Life, like a steps;

We danced as couple,
We Rome like lovers,
We climb like climbers,
We hide, we gossip, we chat, we worry,
About each other,

All the fun and things are done by us,
We never create stories alone,
We create stories for you and me for both of us,
We create poems for those , who could get fall in love;

It just like childhood we grown up, then to teenager ,
And then to college life starts,
But that's not enough,
We have to go through life lessons, and aspects,

Which complete the poem by joining the lines,

TWENTY-ONE
TWENTY

Life is like carnival of joy that leap,
Hearts are like billions of storms to deep,

Boys and girls are smart & strong,
The time comes and goes,
The waves of love going to explore,

The time is fast, as youngster are smart,
Some creates the history, some creates the art,
Everyone as unique as there part,

Some got depressed, some gonna enjoys the journey,
Some remember the days of hostel Life in a college life,
Some being the men as earlier they was,

Every taste of life comes and goes,at age of 20,
Some of them broke the heart, some of them bind the heart,
Some of them still alone, some of them gonna addicts of
unusual things,

Some of them dream big, some of them just want to pass,

Some of them ,just come for heart,
Some of them just, want the art,
Some of them with high's and lows,

It doesn't matter but though some are tall and small,some
them old or new,
But this life teaches of nature to learn,

We learn at last, there is noone behind us,
Only we to us and then left alone is the I,
That is myself, alone , can win ;

TWENTY-TWO
THE OWL HOOTS AS I SING A SONG

The poetry of the earth is never dead,
As i sing a song a owl come and sit on tree,

When I started with my lyrical part,
The owl Hoots as long as he could,
The neighbour came and saw a owl Hoots at night,
As a reality shows it get start's,

I sang the song, o captain! O captain! O captain!
Come here we both sing a song of a sail,
We both, we both are men,
I could you should, we both can says thing's can be done,

We are one, we are long, we can make a song,
We are not,we are not , we are not get afraid of anyone,
We touch, we touch to the ground of success,
We are sailor,a sailor not pirates to raid,

Our journey is awesome with full of adventure as bird says,

As vowels is ready to make us a fame,

TWENTY-THREE

NOTHING MATTERS

Nothing matters of something just befallen unduly,
And often would reshape in word,

Not the love leave behind,
Nor the promises are remained forever,
Nor any races are confined,
Nor any faces are inclined,

Nothing matters if you lost in journey,
Nothing matters if you lost in the race,
Nothing matters if you lost in exams,
Nothing matters if you lost in life,

If not succeeded it not comes with you in death,
And the things be heavy on you,
Not the way leaved quite and worrying,

All the above is nothing matters nor the marks in these wild future,

Nor any paper can decide our future,

All the things in your hand, no need to worry for marks,
Coz , if you learn the skills you, can choose your destiny take
a fly and fly high,
Till you not reach to your destiny,
Then all the marks, paper nothing matters in your life ,

All the things are be happy and never judge yourself with
others,
Nor compare with others, coz you are unique in your way
and style,

You deserve greater than this people who lost in book,
With every line reciting, you deserve greater than this one,

TWENTY-FOUR

A COUNTRY FEEDER

"There is nothing matters in life, coz life is a chance of lord"

"Life is a culture of work, power and field of success in agriculture"

Walk miles and miles in barren field,
Bare footed, don't feel the sting,
Empty tummy, heart filled with zeal,
Smile on face and soul filled with dream,

Making every footsteps as evergreen,
When seeds putted getting a bean,
To feed the country with nutrients of beta carotene,
To make healthy to everyone with bottle gourd as figurine,

Sun over head, body wrapped in moistures,

Cloister with cows work, continuously in fields,
Wind blows fiercely, thou stand steadily,
Walk miles, and smiles in the barren field,

The seeds are born newly, by preparing the fields,
Were sky is ready to bliss water in fields,

A caretaker and backbone of our country,
With caring others, feeding others,
But still,there is noone to say,
Proudly we say that life is all about Agriculture

TWENTY-FIVE
A WINTER

I' ve never known to snowy winter that in poems,
Or the winter that make news,

But winter is frosty, fiery sleepy heads,
Blinks an hour or two,then,
A yellow -red sun, set again,

Again the star comes and hold the skies long,
At the morning there is the dark in the sun,got hide in the
clouds,

There was shivering of body from every angle,
And cold breeze enter through the small gap of my house,

The snow cover the roads, the tree looks as white pearl,
With white blanket, of pearl all the city hampers,

The winter appears frosty cold, and there is a white blanket
appears in the ground,

TWENTY-SIX

LITTLE JOY

I recognise that true, happiness isn't something large &
looming on the horizon ahead,
but small , numerous & already here the warm sunset,

Smile of someone,the love, beautiful face,
Your matching clothes, your
Wierd behaviour,

There will be a little movements, and another obstacles to
overcome,
More danger are horizon,
That's life,

But there is more lessons to come in life than conquering
the victorious mountain,
Relax once in a while,
Your success is meaningless without little joy,

TWENTY-SEVEN
WRITER

I am your story, you are my writer,
I am your prologue, you are my creator's,
You are of peace, i am of anger,

You hold the storm, i am being to stop,
You are my screenplay, i am your actor,
You be the dialogues, i will be the screen,

You will be the writer, I will be your story
You will be the creator, i will be your universe,
You will be the nature, i will be the forest

TWENTY-EIGHT
NAVIGATES

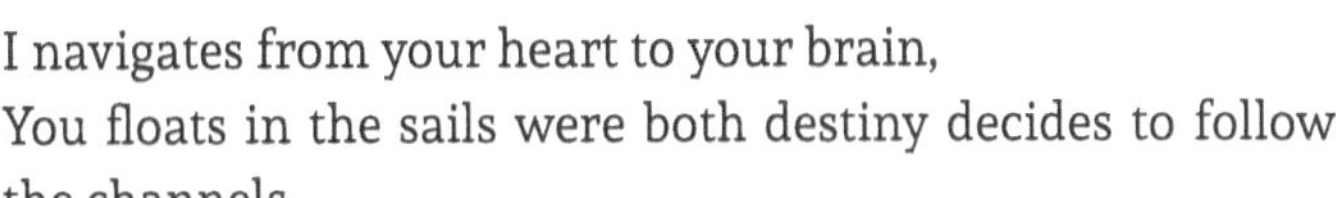

I navigates from your heart to your brain,
You floats in the sails were both destiny decides to follow
the channels,

No one, can create hate and differences
in the smooth sail,
The journey offshore is never easy,

To reach your heart, i have to pass through storms and
valleys of thunders,

There is the gallons of water, which reaches to you,
Which ask the canopy of shadows,
To calm the sun & rise the darkness
To restore the heart to be your part again,

TWENTY-NINE
PRAYER

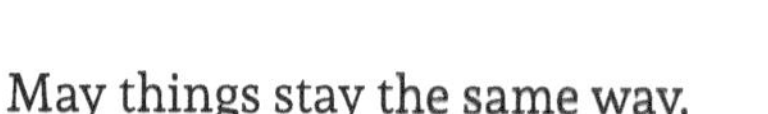

May things stay the same way,
They are as simplest as you know,

May the shuttered windows keep the air cool as spring
brings the flower to you,
May the fragrance of room with the lovers breathe,

May nothing be distributed in simplest place ,
You know for you there is a wanderlust,

In free air were your footprints being recognised a blue
print splits in the soil,
And it get dissolved by sand,

May poem begin with clustering of twigs & sunrays,
Faith should spread amongst all,

May the sun, should carry millions of rays,
Which touching to your heart, carry love,hope & magic to
you,

May the prayer brings joy, prosperous life to everyone im these world;

THIRTY
THE LOST MAN

To reach the pole you have to go far beyond miles distance,

From bewildering sun, to the little fern in the moist ,
From the moist to the cool areas were the light turns to
darkness,

From the darkness to the ages of lights,
Were the sun never reaches only the presence of dark,

Were no one is present,only the snow and men in dark,
Were single owl and fox sit under the tree,
Were there is no sun, only cold wind and frozen breeze in
the air,

To reach the pole you have to go far beyond,
The humans were noone live only dead ones with peace,
sorrows
And small white flowers,

THIRTY-ONE
WHY??

My eyes burns, as i see the clouds from the room,
The beard grows long as it decides to be grown,

I can't decide what is happening to me,
Maybe due to the memories with her,
Or maybe the time I have spent with you was wrong?
Maybe ,i have never been meet to you,

May be the dark clouds set that day and we never meet that day,
As that day was raining,

I don't understand now a days whether it is night or day is going on,
Or the hours are going fast,
Or whether I loose myself with hope of frost,

My mind was frenzy of emotions and hatred,
Towards myself I was ruin completely,

There was no emotions which were laying me, out of these

world,
Go out , check yourself?

The negativity spread inside me was abundance,

Eyes was red with hatred and full of revenge,

Tears were stopped coz, you gave me worst lessons of my
life,

My sorrows, twittered and told me,
"Why to waste time for one"?

There are thousands are waiting for you to be perfect,
To come and knock the door ,
And say that to another, that better luck, next time??

THIRTY-TWO

I WOULD LOVE YOU THOUSANDS OF TIMES

I would love you thousands of times,
When you give up your every hope,
I would hold you as you go down the slope,
I would love you in a hell also if you wish to me to go,
I would love you in struggle ,
When you achieve your aim,

I would walk with you in that freezing cold,
I would always be the hand, when you wanna hold,
I would be sunrise, you will be sunset to me,
I will be the cosmos, you will be the nature to hold,

I would love to live in the shadows of your air,
I would love to be drowned , in the depth of your despair,

I will love you from the sunrise to setting down of sun,
I will love you in every moments before it gone,

I will love you more than my heart beat,

I will love you my girl, through my life upto the death

THIRTY-THREE
TO BREAK AGAIN

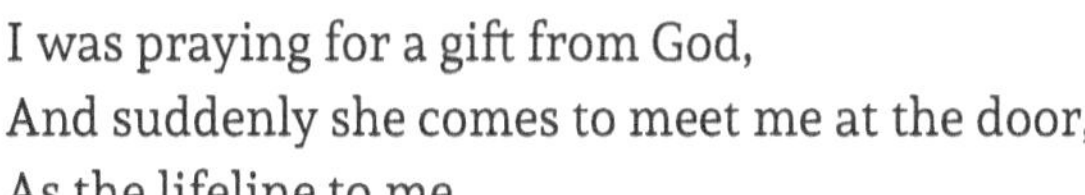

I was praying for a gift from God,
And suddenly she comes to meet me at the door,
As the lifeline to me,

She saved me from the darkness and sorrows,
She solved all the problems which I have faced,
She put me in a place where no one can replace,

She held my hand at lowest time,
And walked with me to go further,

When I was silent as grave she gave me a voice to raise high,

It's inevitable everything goods come to an end,
She might got me from the way,
But then realised,
That she has saved me, just to break again

THIRTY-FOUR
THE HILLS COVERED WITH SNOW

The Hill covered with snow ,
Young mighty stromtroopers of our land,
Secure our hills,
Being pride with flag, and power to devote life,

The bridge glore with happiness to shade the hill with colour red,

To dig the drenches in the grounds,
To kill the enemies and put the bodies down,
Our land is creator for all,
We are the protector of our country,

Which neither been taken by any enemy,
We are toughest and brave to hold the country strong,
We will never bow head, down,
We would raise head high above the clouds,

As dear could not touch to us,
We will fly high above the grounds,
Were there is open air and mountain to go and fly,

We are the warrior which protects the hill from top-notch,
We are the survival, we are the rider of our country,
WE are the heart, we are the soul of our land,

THIRTY-FIVE
IN THE SEARCH OF YOU

I have travelled across the space, in the dwarf planets and mighty constellations,

I have seen the cosmos, present inside you,
Telling literal stories of space & beyond life,

I have seen flower blooming in the space,
Create a magical world to you,

Thou, we are not United, but get unite soon,
You may not understand due to the life,

Coz...
I am beyond life, were millions of ages you have to pass,

To learn how we grow,
How we create the universe??

THIRTY-SIX

INEVITABILITIES

I find single most remarkable thing about love is the way it
is doomed to pain
& loss from
it's onset

Whether it is spouse that outlines their lover
Or looses them to another there is no escaping this most
Solemn
Of
Inevitabilities...

THIRTY-SEVEN
A LOST DREAM

When the morning were simple and the evening were gold
& yellow;

When the conversation would draw,
On for hours , and hours in all,

The spaces between us is wild as horizon,
When oceans could not divide the dream
A moment of eye contact
Could
Outshine the sun,

While I may live beneath the shadow of your love,

We once shared our journey under the vale of stars, in the
dark open night,
With no clouds and clear vision,

There is a light that shines even here,

Constellations comes together,

To complete the couplet of prose ,
That join the hymns and rhymes with you,

THIRTY-EIGHT
HAPPY HEART

A love cannot simply measured in months, or years,

It's quality of the measures that matter,

The secret thing about happy heart is complex,
Matter

But the simple answer is
To enjoy

Everything while it last

THIRTY-NINE
WINTER BIRDS

Winter comes singing song from the dead leaves,
To the top of the trees,
Where the wind pushes the branches,

The forest & wind plays ,
Birds help in charming the day with chirp,chirp,

Each flowers bloom & grow
In the weather full of snow,
Putting up some sugar flakes,
All the beams shine together,

The bird spell the white colour,
To cherry red, to the cherry green,
Giving expression of leaf , tree and snow,

The bird sing a song of winter,
To come and bless everyone to grow strong,
Everything can grow tall and big of the winter comes,

FORTY

THE NIGHT IN L.A.

Light strokes writhing knot tying light paths,
Calligraphy of cars,
With basin & hill tops,

Wilshire tower at the west of Missippi,
The hunting library with beautiful skyscrapers,

Sun goes calm in the beaches with lighthouse,
The chaotic street, with palm trees,

West side the sant Monica hills,
And downtown as City Central,

The sand stone & beauty of flower adores the jewels of the
night,
With lights, foodies and coconut paslm,
In the night at L.A.

FORTY-ONE
DAWN

Far away at top of the hills there was light,

I can see it clear through my weakened sight,
Unseen trees sway in cool midnight breeze,
In a sea of black failing to cease,

I am a tiny drop in the endless sea,
I do not glow like that light i see,

Though my eyes twinkle like a feeble stars,

Gazing lazily for hours & hours,
The light is steady , it does not flicker,
but dawn approaches as fast as quicker,
And soon the unwavering light is done,

Consumed by the brilliance of the shinning sun,

FORTY-TWO
HIBERNATION

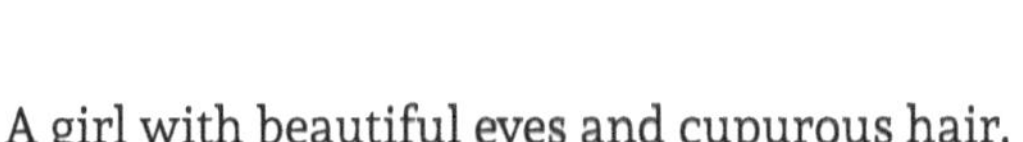

A girl with beautiful eyes and cupurous hair,
Has almost disappeared, from the Brooke
Under the snow,

Blurred consciousness called her away,
From the winter world,

But still she faintly distinguished, the grey
Sky & thin ghosts of the trees,

It didn't matter, she wanted to get out
Of the cold,
Persistently kissed her face ,her numb hands &
She silently took the care until she dissolved into the white
void of winter sleep,

FORTY-THREE
THE KINGDOMS

The kingdoms are mellow, titles
With oak, Aspen, willow & rosewood,

Or the snow, for which the people of North
Have dozens of stories to describe different arrivals,

The creatures with their thick,
Fur , their shy & wordless graze,

Their infallible sense of what their lives, are meant to be,

The world grow rich, grows wild ,and you too,

Grow rich, grow sweet and wild ,
With ecstasy of flowers and chirping birds,

FORTY-FOUR
DEATH

Why people afraid of death?

You never knew it & you never know ,
Life is joy, life is suffering,
While death is a light filled show,

I am not king of death,
I am only just a boy,
And in my questions to the masters,
I ve understood that death means to destroy,

Destroying your earthly clothes,
Is the surface meanings of death,
The destruction of ego,
Is what happens when you pause the breathe.,

It is life to the Nirvana,
Were there is soul which is immortal ,only the body is dead,

The soul meets to the concept of life that is death,
It passes from the stage to the new creation of new body for

the soul,

So life is a cycle ,if we die , we born again
In another life , but we forget everything that we have to
remember,

FORTY-FIVE

HUNGER

I have seen hunger from my closet eye,
Though by other name told by all,

No one, listen about your story, your cry,
Your sin,
All passes by keeping you in unfit conditions,

Nor even , the rice, nor even the piece of bread is given to
you,
Only the day with struggle & night with cry as gifted to you,

Every eclipses comes with wisdoms & praises,
It brings lofty food to you,

Uttered words are simple to tell,
But a life of a man is struggle , it couldn't not fail,
It always teaches the lesson, and dump you in the land,
From where you have , grown,

FORTY-SIX
WHAT IS LOVE ?

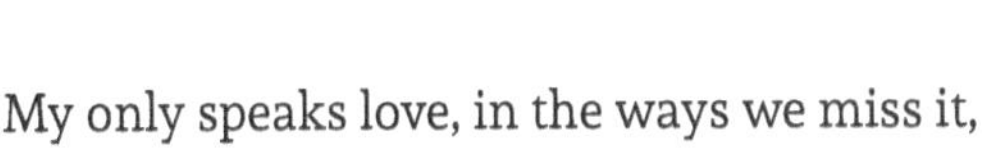

My only speaks love, in the ways we miss it,
Sometimes in Nature's lap,
Or the stars so brightly lit,

The Heart sees love is a purest form,
Although love is always pure,
But these pretty eyes, binded now can see this god no more,

Sun shades and rain drops,
Falling on the lovely earth,
The night goes into peaceful slumber,
A new life, everyday takes a new birth,

Squirrels jump, and run freely,
Hugging the trees , rolling to ground,
In those beautiful moments of freedoms,
As the love splits in the air,

Love is as aroma splashed around a millions different forms,

The whopping wind, the blooming flower
Or in my solitude,amidst the storms,

Love can never be achieved,
Neither can it be stolen or broken,
Love is like a river with millions of emotions,

A journey that is chosen it is never ending,

The universe will spread happiness inside you,
When you love someone,

FORTY-SEVEN

THE INDIAN SUMMERS

I saw my days passionate with playing algorithms &
integers,

They leaped with the wind as leaves,
Leaping upon the wind to flow like a kites,

It is the season of my mellowest appetite
With beautiful bud and Astonishing breeze,

The breathe heals the pain, and give comfort,
With water,hills and forest make a new adventure,
As Indian summer with full of joyful avenues,
With new day and new adventure,

A new sunshine with a cool wind ,
Assert the kingdom with autumn falls,

FORTY-EIGHT

I HAVE READ NOVELS

I have read a good number of novels in my life,
Most of them claimed that love is the centre of universe,

It is where everything falls apart and everything comes together,

Love is what the universe depends on to exist,
And after the novels,I read,I never actually understand it,
until the time decided by her,

I never know what it feels like to see someone and smile for no reason,
I never knew how to turn my anger to love,
I never thought so deeply of another soul,
It all happened , when another person enters to my life,

She held , my hand led me out of darkness,
Your past can be painful yet satisfying,

I never knew I 'm capable of love is so pure,
I never looked at the moon& fet like I do now,

I never looked at the moon but it felt now,
I never know there is so much love inside me can make me
different,

FORTY-NINE

HOW MANY TIMES??

How many times the word you write
Break & destroy you,
Before they heal you,

How many times,
You swallow the ink,
Before pouring it ,
On your healing wounds,

How many times,
You try to count aches,
But confused with numbers of words,

How many times
While writing about you,
Seen the page,
That Love in the Air,

How many times,

You walk searching
For a half buried poem,
Coz, it looks like you,

How many times,
You think there is a way,
To return or maybe to escape ,
But the words of your,
Own poems blocks you,

How many times,
You compromise yourself
Or to heal your wound,
By writing paragraphs of your choice,

How many times,
The words will be sharp the nail of swords,
To cut the view,
Where no one deserves,

FIFTY

A Thousand Splendid Sun

A beautiful shrines encircled with mountains,
And valley with rivers ousted the rhymes of your eyes,

The beauty of the trees & beauty of her lips,
Enbounded with charisma of greeness,

You spread the sparkling blush in the environment,
The sun is here to spread thousands of encircled shape,
To see the beauty of your appearance,

The nature alofted you a gift of sun,
To enshrined your beauty in all world,

FIFTY-ONE
DEPLETED SOUL

I have been holding onto you,
For far too long my dear,

I have been holding onto the dream,
We once shared out of love out of fear,

And it has become synonymous with
the perpetual state of my depleted soul,

For I have been holding onto you,
For far too long my dear,

This agony needs an end,
For it has become synonymous,
With the perpetual state of my
Already depleted soul,

I wish I knew a ways to summarise the infinite that resides
in me,
The infinite kingdom that you make for both of us,

FIFTY-TWO
ONE MORE DEATH

I do not know why, but it seems
Lately my heart, has been trying to tell me something,

It almost feels as though there is another death that my
heart must go through,

Perhaps it was he was foretold, predestined, the journey of
both our these two hearts were never meant to be forever,

I do not know why it almost feels, as though,
there's just on more time this heart must go through one
more death,

FIFTY-THREE

THE DREAM WILL CONTINUE WITH YOU

I read somewhere,that we should stop,
Chasing the dreams that are not made for us,

That we must learn how to go of things,
That are not meant for us,

That we must accept our fate, for sometimes,
We are not always meant to get
What the heart yarns far,

So I stopped reading together with stories,

For I am believer ,
For I am on a leap of faith,
And I will chase this dream
Till the end of my time,

For I am also an avid dreamer
And
The dream my dear,
Is always going to be you,

FIFTY-FOUR

A BEAUTIFUL HEARTACHE

I had a thought today, amongst many other thoughts,

And in that thought I was just holding her
With her head on my chest & staying still,

And she asks - what are you doing?
I , keeping my eyes closed , very softly whispered,

I am finally resting,

FIFTY-FIVE

IF ONE LEFT FIRST

Remember when we imagine what one of us ,
Would do, if the other left first,

How would we argue over waiting be the first one to leave,
for we knew we couldn't bear the departure,

We were right, for now I lives an empty shell of a man once
filled to the brine of love & hope,

So I often wonder why did he put his love,
Inside of me, embed it so deep,
inside my heart,

If he had always known,
How it was never meant for me to keep,

FIFTY-SIX
WATERFALL

O beauty of perennial ages, as thou stream down tors,
I behold thou sail, enthralled by the roar,
As to the time , thy arms sway and fume Aan ivory of horse,
Gushing down the serendipity to reach the final shore,

For thou, choosest each road that no man has ever taken,
And createst thou new land , to inhabitable floors,
They begotten Brooks a million ebony mounts have broken,
O beauty of perennial ages ,as thou stream down tors ,

Thither afar the peak shines, aureate shades gleam bright,
Thou too as begotten child ; scurry to make new shores,
O for miles thou stream and stream for days through nights,
I behold though sail, enthralled by roar,

Thou in charms sail forth, bewitching men around,
For, thy beauty must thrive along, through thou course,
Feedest thou thirsty soul and those starving hounds,
As to the time thy arms sway and fume as ivory of horse,

The trenches art too deep, thou deluge as gleeful stream
And thousands eyes thy splendidness adore,
For a few moments lone, i behold thou as a dream,
Gushing down in serendipity to reach the final shore

FIFTY-SEVEN
HUMAN BEING

There is nothing more relaxing
than the present
Moment,

Just right here,
nowhere else,

For once do not linger,
in the past,
do not look the future,
do not face
the facts
since they will
make you think,

Leave it
Let it be,
The Mind becomes
So full
We forget
that it is open,

As human beings
No need, to worry about all events
happening in life,
Just relax, chill and enjoy the movement;

FIFTY-EIGHT
WHEN I MET POETRY

For my love,
I store you in my poems,
And in the chambers of my heart;

For my life,
A ghost of the losses,
And the journey from the sun to the moon,
And all the beautiful parts,

When I met poetry,
I have seen you in my dreams,
The dream empires the destination,

And your
Poetry have driven,
The world with beautiful Amber

FIFTY-NINE
HOPE

I hope you find someone with whom,
You can once again gaze upon the night,
Sky filled with stars,

I hope you find someone, who would light up your day,
And I accept you with all your scars;

I hope you find someone, who would give you the butterflies
you once felt with me around,

I hope you find , someone who'd be your cover,
Be your shelter who'd hold you up and keep you
Safe who'd make you the jewel on his crown,

For I need you to put and end to this,
For I know I cannot stop the pain that resides,
Within me from being in love with you, every
Walking moment;

But I know for sure the ease& comfort,
I can create for those who love me just being okay;

SIXTY

THE SUN AND THE MELTED MOON

Dear sun never rise in horizon,
Let us taste the night to the fullest,

It's mysterious silent and sensouousness,

The melted piece of moon in bluish plate,
With sun and the warm rays,

It heated the earth but create the brightness,
And give birth to new ones,

It might be small herbs or might be shrubs,
But the world glows as you arrives

SIXTY-ONE

LOVED ONES ....
MY MOTHER!

Mother's are precious.....
The gem which are priceless .....
Cannot return their favour & love....
The choice is only to be their in debt....

The truth of my life is,
Without her I am nothing in this whole world,

She is my strength,
My soul is hers,
Drifted from the heaven,
And she is with me since I have born,

Life without mother
Is never been better,
If you lose your mother,
You can't have another,

She is like a flower,

She never cries ever,
In my life she is a teacher,
Who teaches me forever,

She is also person who have the difficulties,
But she never , told about anything;
Always, with smile & happiness;
She overcome with situation,

Ocean of emotions I discover,
With its wave I feel better,
Just a smile of your mother,
Make you in paradise live forever,

The words are less to say about mother,
Coz, she is special, she is a heaven, she is a universe,
Who given a birth to a pearl,
She is a universe to me, which can't be described in words
or few sentences;

SIXTY-TWO
FEELINGS FOR LOVED ONES

None else can understand the importance of family,
Ask an orphan, and he definitely tell you the story,
How his mother died, while he was small and protecting it,
And how is father died,by feeding the family and himself
lost in hunger ;

The garland of smiles one can wear,
living with the family,
Anything can be solved, when parents live in reality,
Laughter and smile can be exchanged around,
And fights occur smoothly, but patch seems so profound,

Just like hub of trees, with many fruits dangling on it,
A family blooms perfectly, when all members exists,
No one can rely on, only family help in tough times,
Rest come and go, but family is remembered for lifetime,

Ain't good to know that there are people to understand,
Someone waits for you at home, and cook meal with

affection,
Such is the importance of a family,
Which only few understand,
The old age homes are misery and a bad part to comprehend,

So family is the home of joy,
Never make sad or sorrow to anyone,
Coz, they love you, they care you,
They do everything for you,
Coz they are family;

9 798886 410846